100

THINGS TO DO IN

ATHENS, GA

BEFORE YOU

DIE

The Arch at the University of Georgia

100

THINGS TO DO IN

ATHENS, GA

BEFORE YOU

DIE

• •

JUDY & LEN GARRISON

REEDY PRESS

Library of Congress Control Number: 2022936982

ISBN: 9781681063775

Design by Jill Halpin

All images were provided by Seeing Southern LLC, Len Garrison.

Printed in the United States of America
22 23 24 25 26   5 4 3 2 1

We (the publisher and the author) have done our best to provide the most accurate information available when this book was completed. However, we make no warranty, guarantee, or promise about the accuracy, completeness, or currency of the information provided, and we expressly disclaim all warranties, express or implied. Please note that attractions, company names, addresses, websites, and phone numbers are subject to change or closure, and this is outside of our control. We are not responsible for any loss, damage, injury, or inconvenience that may occur due to the use of this book. When exploring new destinations, please do your homework before you go. You are responsible for your own safety and health when using this book.

DEDICATION

To all those who love Athens, these 100 things are merely a beginning to the adventures this city offers. Keep the love affair going strong, and now and forever, "Go Dawgs!"

• •

The Ice Dawgs

CONTENTS

• •

Music and Entertainment

Sports and Recreation

• •

Culture and History

• •

PREFACE

I've had a lifelong love affair with the Classic City. As a child, my parents and I jumped in the sedan and sprinted from the North Georgia Mountains to Athens to visit family. It thrilled me because of McDonald's—the mountains didn't have those. Then, as a college junior, I made the transition from a tiny junior college in the mountains to the grandest college stage imaginable.

The University of Georgia (UGA) intimidated me, but it didn't take me long to fall in love. In the 1970s, the downtown was just big enough to get lost in, and farmland still decorated the countrysides. Every Athenian screamed, "How 'Bout Them Dawgs!" and the B & L Warehouse rocked all night long with live music.

Today, not much has changed, only the scale. The campus remains the city's calling card, and music raises rafters most nights.

Athens is not only the UGA campus but also thriving neighborhoods, award-winning restaurants, inspirational art galleries, greenways, and gardens.

Inside, we'll introduce you to this foodie town, featuring chefs' unique interpretations of southern cuisine. The music scene never lost a beat, with continued favor for local stars. Dives and bars, pubs and restaurants, cinemas and cafés invite everyone to walk the menagerie of streets. There isn't a thing you can't find here.

• •

If the outdoors beckons, the city parks and greenways open the land with bicycle trails and hiking.

And, of course, you haven't lived until you are between the hedges of Sanford Stadium as the Dawgs battle on Dooley Field. Len and I are thrilled to share our hometown. As travel journalists and photographers, we have covered the world through imagery and words, yet no location is as inspiring or vibrant to us as Athens.

Enjoy your adventures. If you fall in love and stay, we'll welcome you with open arms.

Café Racer Coffee + Donuts

FOOD AND DRINK

EAT A BLUE-PLATE SPECIAL IN THE PICASSO ROOM
AT FIVE AND TEN

From a weekly blue-plate special to the finest wines from southern Italy and the Loire Valley in France, dining at Five and Ten feels like coming home. It's the 100-year-old Hawthorne House that welcomes diners for chef-curated creations Monday through Saturday. James Beard Award–winning chef Hugh Acheson opened Five and Ten, his flagship restaurant, in 2000 in the Five Points neighborhood. It has been and remains a community-driven restaurant, creating foods that offer a taste for everyone. With a seasonal menu inspired by local farmers, the traditional southern cuisine takes a European turn with French and Italian influences that Acheson learned during his early years in Canada. The weekly chef-designed blue-plate special is comfort food at its best: possibly chicken-fried steak with collard greens. Start with the pimento cheese with bacon marmalade. Revel in great food and drink, and be happy. It's that simple.

1073 S Milledge Ave., 706-546-7300
fiveandten.com

TIP
Reservations are recommended through Open Table.

SAY YES TO COOKIE DOUGH
AT ALUMNI COOKIE DOUGH

Never tell a woman "No" to cookie dough.

Entrepreneur Jennifer Dollander was a closet cookie dough eater. After being inspired by a cookie dough café in New York City, Dollander began working on her own recipe in her home kitchen with her kids as taste-testers. This University of Georgia alumna crafted dough with consistency and safety paramount. Not only can you eat it raw, but you can also bake it. The best of both worlds, it's a childhood miracle. Within six months, Alumni Cookie Dough opened in its downtown location. Small batches are made daily. Have a cookie dough sandwich, a scoop in a cup or a cone, or a milkshake. Student Study Survival Packs aid during finals. Favorites like cookies and cream, peanut butter surprise, or freshman fifteen create a party in your mouth. Available in vegan, gluten friendly, and keto options.

480 N Thomas St., 706-254-9171
alumnicookiedough.com

TIP
Take cookie dough to the next level by adding ice cream

DRINK BEER AND GET STUFF
ON THE ATHENS BEER TRAIL

This all-American town is becoming a beer town. In addition to education, food, and football, it's adding beer to its list of national honors. With six breweries within the city limits, following the trail makes for a great afternoon or weekend of craft brew exploration. Local restaurants take pride in serving local brews, but experiencing the breweries allows you not only to order flights to taste and determine your favorite, but also to hang out with friends in the beer garden. And with the inception of the Beer Trail, there's free stuff. It's as easy as this: walk into a bar (at any of the listed breweries), announce that you're following the Athens Beer Trail, and you'll receive an official Athens Beer Trail Field Guide. Then visit a brewery and receive a stamp. After six stamps, head to the Welcome Center for an authentic Beer Trail mug. You're an official member of the Athens Brew Crew.

CHEERS TO ATHENS!

Normaltown Brewing Co.
Small-batch, New England–style brews
Thursday–Sunday
149 Oneta St., 6B2, 706-850-8996
normaltown-brewing-co.business.site

Southern Brewing Company
Seasonal brews
Wednesday–Sunday
231 Collins Industrial Blvd., 706-548-7183
sobrewco.com

Creature Comforts Brewing
Be comfortable with favorites like Athena and Classic City Lager
Monday–Sunday
271 W Hancock Ave., 706-410-1043
creaturecomfortsbeer.com

Akademia Brewing Company
Brewpub serving lunch and dinner with brews accompanied by
Six-String Therapy
Monday–Sunday
150 Crane Dr., 678-726-2288
akademiabc.com

Athentic Brewing Company
Freshman brewery in Normaltown
Wednesday–Sunday
108 Park Ave.
athenticbrewing.com

Terrapin Beer Co.
Favorite Hopsecutioner plus hemp-infused sours and stouts
Monday–Sunday
265 Newton Bridge Rd., 706-549-3377
terrapinbeer.com

START WITH A SIDE OF GEORGIA PEACH FRENCH TOAST
AT MAMA'S BOY

Mama's Boy is quintessential Athens. Born in an old laundromat, this retro diner speaks to everything that is beautiful about Athens. Hospitality. Service. Community. The original plan 15 years ago was to open for dinner only. With its location not being in one of the best locations in Athens, people didn't come. The owners changed the restaurant into a breakfast spot, and it was business gold. Located just off the North Oconee Greenway, the original location wakes for breakfast with baking sheets of hot biscuits and homemade raspberry jam that's as expected on the table as salt and pepper. The restaurant serves breakfast and lunch, but it's the breakfast that creates the line long before the doors open. Traditional southern fare like biscuits and gravy with unexpected favorites like pulled-pork tacos and salmon cakes Benedict are made daily from seasonal local products. They even concede to chocolate cake and cinnamon buns for breakfast.

Downtown Athens: 197 Oak St., 706-548-6249

Falls of Oconee: 8851 Macon Hwy., Ste. 403, 706-850-8550

mamasboyathens.com

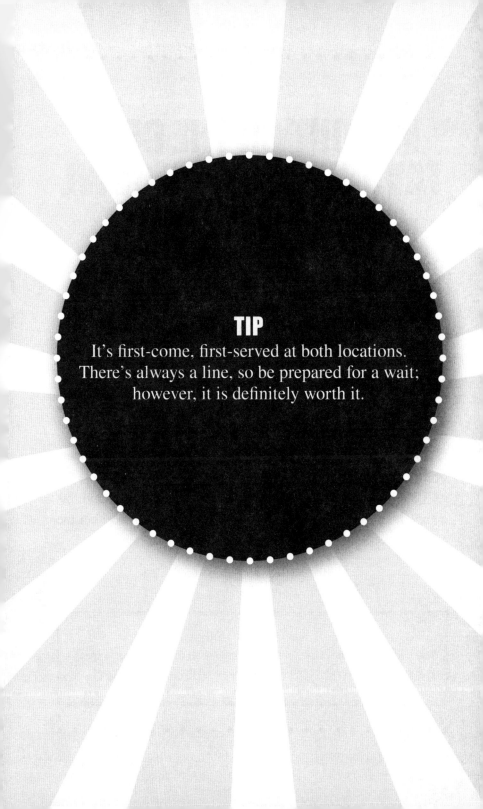

TIP

It's first-come, first-served at both locations. There's always a line, so be prepared for a wait; however, it is definitely worth it.

VEG OUT ON THE CULT-FAVORITE GOLDEN BOWL
AT THE GRIT

The Grit has been a staple in Athens for over two decades, serving vegetarian dishes to those who claim the distinction and to those who simply like good food and lots of it. Located in a historic building with peeling paint and red-light-district history, the staff understands that not everyone gets the vegan thing or the tofu thing. So, they season heavily with garlic, onions, and such, that provides the kick in the pants. There's a chance you'll even forget that tofu is in the bowl—that is, if it's not your thing. It's casual and relaxed dining with a chalkboard of daily specials. The seating area is small and a few outside tables are available, with a bird's-eye view of the comings and goings on Prince Avenue. The Grit honors the music scene with devotion to the musicians that helped build this eatery. It's rumored that Michael Stipe is part owner of either the restaurant or building; that's another reason to be a regular.

199 Prince Ave., 706-543-6592
thegrit.com

TIP
The 20th anniversary Grit cookbook contains all their favorite recipes. A portion of proceeds benefits Nuci's Space, a nonprofit health and music resource center in Athens.

CARVE INTO A FILET MIGNON
AT PORTERHOUSE GRILL

Are you in the mood for steak? Step into Porterhouse Grill. Casual fine dining at its best, Porterhouse Grill anchors the downtown eating experience with meat perfection. Jaw-dropping dishes prepared with skill and time draw locals in time and again. Take a seat at the marble bar with a window view of the city, or cozy up in a booth in the dining room. The menu isn't packed with unique or trendy dishes but with standards that people have come to know and appreciate from the finest of steakhouses. Fine wines by the glass or bottle are available to complete the culinary experience; allow the host to select the perfect pairing. From salads to fresh fish to choice cuts of beef, dinner is a satisfying experience topped off by delicious and drinkable desserts. Discover one of the most extensive drink menus available in town. Specialty cocktails include Georgia's own Richland Rum.

459 E Broad St., 706-369-0990
porterhouseathens.com

TIP
Make reservations on the website.

TAKE YOUR COFFEE AT DRIVE-BY TRUCKERS TRUCKER SPEED
AT JITTERY JOE'S

It's the only place in Athens where orange is an acceptable color choice. Celebrity clientele like Michael Stipe of R.E.M. and the B-52s helped make the orange cup of joe an Athens staple. In its beginnings, its location next door to the 40 Watt Club kept coffee pouring all hours of the night for concertgoers, as well as for anyone who burned the midnight oil. In 1994, Jittery Joe's copyrighted the name, reduced the hours, and roasted the beans in small batches to fill the bright orange cup. Their cup of java is surpassed only by the creative, limited-edition, 12-ounce cans, filled with whole beans or medium grind. Each colorful, collectible can and its title pays homage to the city of Athens, its musical heritage, and the best collections of coffee available.

FUN FACT
Once the official coffee of Antarctica, Jittery Joe's was named one of the top 24-hour coffeehouses in America by *Rolling Stone* magazine.

JITTERY JOE'S LOCATIONS

Downtown roaster tasting room
425 Barber St., 706-227-2161

297 E Broad St., Downtown, 706-613-7449

1230 S Milledge Ave., Five Points, 706-208-1979

1480 Baxter St., 706-548-1099

1860 Barnett Shoals Rd., 706-354-8000

1880 Epps Bridge Pkwy., #101, 706-354-8900

27 Greensboro Hwy., Watkinsville, 706-769-4280

jitteryjoes.com

TIP

Look for the ESP Java Joy van around town. Joyristas serve Jittery Joe's coffee in many pop-up locations. The nonprofit Extra Special People (ESP) allows adults with disabilities to pour the coffee and provide the smiles. You'll never forget this cup of coffee.

ESPRESSO YOURSELF!

1000 Faces Coffee
510 N Thomas St.
706-534-8860
1000facescoffee.com

Molly's Coffee Company
8830 Macon Hwy.
762-499-2002
mollyscoffeeco.com

Hendershots
237 Prince Ave.
706-353-3050
hendershotsathens.com

Bitty & Beau's
1540 S Lumpkin St.
678-361-8184
bittyandbeauscoffee.com

ORDER A CLOCKED!BURGER AND PBJ SHAKE
AT CLOCKED

When a pop band singer marries a modern dancer, it's a match made in creative burger heaven. Since 2001, this Athens duo has crafted burgers that are out of this world. The official mascot, Space Boy, confirms that the burgers, fries, and all the fixings are, indeed, one of a kind. This two-decade-old eatery uses locally sourced ingredients, and everything is cooked to order. Feast on the traditional burger or add a little peanut butter to the mix. What? There's the PeanutButter!Bacon burger. Out of this world, man! There's grilled cheese sandwiches and wieners on brioche buns. Veggie and vegan options are always available. Don't leave without trying a PBJ shake. Order a Dirty Ivan or a Church Lady if you're in the mood for a kick.

259 W Washington St., 706-548-9175
clockeddiner.com

TIP
Sit in the outdoor seating area and take a photo with the whimsical Clocked logo.

SATISFY YOUR SOUL FOOD CRAVINGS
AT WEAVER D'S DELICIOUS FINE FOODS

It's hard to miss the incandescent green building just off the North Oconee Greenway. It's nothing more than a hole-in-the-wall restaurant with about 40 seats, but it has enormous ties to the music world. Dexter Weaver, owner of Weaver D's and this iconic green building, and R.E.M., the Athens-born indie band, go together like mac 'n' cheese. Maryland-born Weaver, who began cooking at age five, made Weaver D's the go-to place for down-home cooking. He delivered fried chicken, pork chops, steak and gravy, plus sweet cornbread, with the uncommon shout of "Automatic for the people"—rather than "You're welcome"—upon serving. When Michael Stipe, lead singer for R.E.M. and a regular customer, asked to use the salutation for their 1992 album, Weaver agreed, and the rest is Grammy music history. Music lovers from all over the world make Weaver D's a destination, whenever they're in Athens.

1016 E Broad St., 706-353-7797

DRINK IN A ROOFTOP VIEW
AT GEORGIA THEATRE OR HYBAR

Athens comes alive at night. As lively as it is during the daylight hours, the lights of the city at night energize the activity. Visit one of two rooftop bars in the city at dusk. Watch the sun go down and wait for the lights to come up. The most famous is atop the Georgia Theatre, with open railings facing the south toward campus and east toward downtown. It offers a full bar and restaurant. The new kid on the block is Hybar at Hyatt Place, which provides a 360-degree view from the hills to Sanford Stadium. They offer cocktails and finger foods plus the Hy-Poppin' Burger. These rooftop bars are within five blocks of each other, so you'll have a chance to visit both in a single evening and decide which is more impressive.

Georgia Theatre
215 N Lumpkin St., 706-850-7670
georgiatheatre.com

Hybar at Hyatt Place
412 N Thomas St., 706-425-1800
hyatt.com

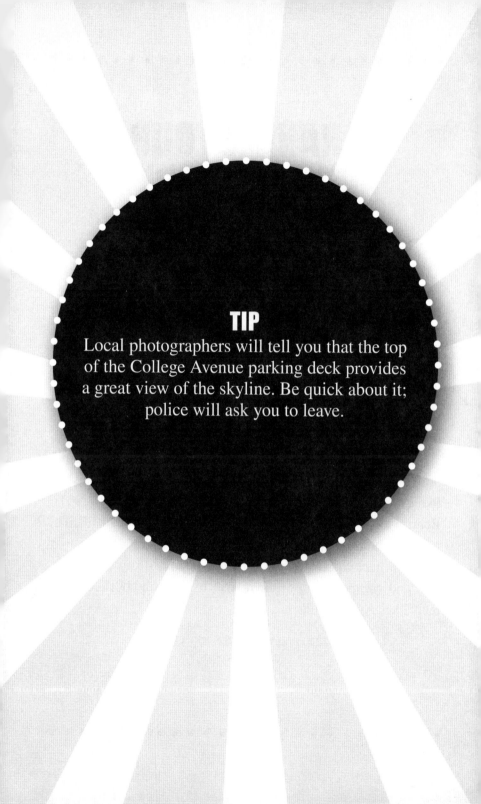

TIP

Local photographers will tell you that the top of the College Avenue parking deck provides a great view of the skyline. Be quick about it; police will ask you to leave.

CHANNEL YOUR INNER GATSBY WITH A COCKTAIL
AT THE OLD PAL

Named after the 1922 rye cocktail crafted by Harry MacElhone in Paris, the Old Pal in the Normaltown community is as welcoming as the cocktails it serves. Think of it as the Athens version of Cheers. Located in a beautiful preserved brick building, its atmosphere is reminiscent of neighborhood meeting places where drinks and conversation drove people inside. Many come to escape the college crowd and sip fancy cocktails that focus on classic style with unique ingredients and fresh garnish. Original house concoctions are produced seasonally alongside classics like Alaskas (1913), Brooklyns (1910), and Airmails (1941). Beer, wine, plus an extensive and unique selection of liquors, are available, but it's the unique craft cocktails that delight. Join them for happy hour from 4 p.m. until 6 p.m. Bring the pooch, too, and escape the downtown rush to the neighborhood that feels like an old friend.

1320 Prince Ave., 706-850-4340
theoldpal.com

HERE'S TO YOU, OL' SPORT

The National
232 W Hancock Ave., 706-549-3450
thenationalrestaurant.com

Butcher & Vine
Kitchen + Wine Bar
1653 S Lumpkin St., 706-850.7767
37 Greensboro Hwy., Watkinsville, 706-705-1466
eatbutcherandvine.com

South Bar + Kitchen
247 E Washington St., Ste. 101, 706-395-6125
southkitchenbar.com

Normal Bar
1365 Prince Ave., 706-648-6186
normaltown.com

The Pine Bar
1235 S Milledge Ave., 706-395-6278
thepineathens.com

DIVE IN
AT ROADHOUSE

Not much larger than the size of an alleyway, Roadhouse bursts at the seams every night of the week with a raucous crowd guzzling Pabst Blue Ribbon and the local brew. The brick walls are plastered with metal beer placards, and neon lights hang over the bar next to the television. If you visit on a Friday or Saturday and a local band takes the six-foot stage, you'll have less room but more friends. The locals arrive early, long before the college kids arrive. The regulars will buy you a drink and initiate hours of pointless conversation. Don't miss regular CC, the 68-year-old local who sits at the corner of the bar every single night. If you see the stool labeled Cadillac Seat, don't sit there. It belongs to CC. Dive bar rules.

137 N Lumpkin St., 706-613-2324

WET YOUR WHISTLE WITH A PEANUTS & COKE COCKTAIL
AT THE PLACE

Go directly upstairs to the bar. Choose a window seat for an ideal glimpse of North Campus and the Arch, and then order a meal that will showcase a new southern culinary experience. The story of this place begins with two UGA graduates and their grandfather's car dealership. It's nicknamed "the Place" because brothers Ryan and Alan want the same welcoming experience at their restaurant as they felt at their grandfather's place. They built their seasonal menu on family recipes and added their own culinary interpretation. Lunch is always a good idea, but it's the dinner menu that shines. Start with black-eyed pea cakes served over collard greens and move to the chicken & waffles with Tabasco-candied bacon strips. Stay awhile and sip the peanuts & Coke cocktail with infused bourbon and its crunchy peanut rim. Its unexpected great taste will spark memories of the last time you emptied a bag of peanuts into your Coke bottle.

229 Broad St., 706-850-2988
theplaceathens.com

RAISE THE HEAT WITH UPTOWN SHRIMP AND A PINEAPPLE JALAPEÑO MARGARITA
AT FIVE ATHENS

Five dinners. Five wines. Five signature cocktails. Five starters that include Uptown shrimp, which make for a great sit-at-the-bar afternoon with friends while cooling the heat with any of the signature cocktails. FIVE calls Birmingham, Mobile, and Tuscaloosa, along with Athens, home. With happy hour every day plus a Thursday ladies' night, FIVE appreciates the call for weekday gatherings. Wine-Down Wednesday makes for the ideal hump day hiatus. Weekends are celebrated with the Saturday and Sunday Jazz Brunch with kicking Bloody Marys. It's all about offering what you need and nothing more. That need continues with American Lunch and Gulf to Table, their nonprofit organizations that feed the needy in every community they call home. FIVE meets need head on.

269 N Hull St., #100, 706-543-5515
five-bar.com

TIP

Partner restaurant Chuck's Fish brings the Gulf Coast to Athens. Fresh fish and traditional sushi rolls are made to order.

chucksfish.com

FIX EVERYTHING
AT OGLETHORPE GARAGE

Part motorcycle garage. Part watering hole. Part food truck stop. What's not to love? Serving fresh local brews at this neighborhood bar, Oglethorpe Garage is a bar/motorcycle co-op that encourages ordering a drink and putting a wrench on your motorcycle at the same time. Don't own a cycle? Come watch the activity from the lounge of the old service station. The young ones are welcome, and several junior moto enthusiasts have broken into their first motors at the shop. The garage was born when the partners hosted bike workshops at their houses. Wanting to create a hub for the growing community, Oglethorpe Garage provides a place to grab a coffee, a cocktail, or food and meet others with the same love of cycles.

1560 Oglethorpe Ave., 706-850-8810

INDULGE IN CREAMY CONFECTIONS
AT CONDOR CHOCOLATES

When Athens meets Ecuador . . . It was a *When Harry Met Sally* moment. When Peter and Nick Dale's American dad met the woman of his dreams while traveling on a bus in Ecuador, it was magic. They married, moved to Athens, and would soon come to satisfy every chocolate lover's obsession. When Nick started making chocolate at home from cacao he brought back from Ecuador, the product became his passion. The entrepreneurial team opened Condor in 2014 and an expanded factory downtown in 2021. This bean-to-bar chocolate company is a total hands-on project, from sourcing the cacao beans to constructing the final product. The Dale team continues to source cacao beans in Ecuador from farmers they know and trust. The downtown factory opens the production process to visitors, so before you make your selection, watch the process. After watching and tasting, feel free to increase your order of truffles and confections.

Downtown Café + Factory
160 E Washington St., 706-521-8966
condorchocolates.com

Five Points Café
1658 S Lumpkin St., 706-850-4803

PRAISE LOCAL FARMERS
AT HEIRLOOM CAFÉ
AND FRESH MARKET

From the produce to the market dishes, the café and market stand on the shoulders of the generations that came before. The family business respects quality food, service, community, and the relationships created as a result of the intersection of the three. They celebrate local famers and tell their stories through the dishes created in the café and the produce available in the market. The market buys from local farmers, including seasonal produce as well as pasture-raised chickens and farm-raised animals. Producers change with the seasons and product availability. The café is open for lunch Tuesday through Friday and supper Wednesday through Saturday. Enjoy a meal created from fresh produce and meats; stop at the market and take home a taste built on multiple generations of the Athens community.

815 N Chase St., 706-354-7901
heirloomathens.com

ENJOY CLASSIC CRAWFISH ETOUFFEE
AT GEORGE'S LOWCOUNTRY TABLE

Savor Louisiana without leaving home. This table has been a go-to in Athens for decades. For the best in Cajun-inspired offerings, George's mantra is "good food, good wine, and good service." Serving an extensive selection of wine by the glass and bottle, this fine-dining experience can begin with crawfish or fried green tomatoes, continue with jambalaya, and finish with bread pudding with bourbon sauce. If oysters are your jam, enjoy by the dozen raw or chargrilled; up the game with Oysters Rockefeller. At the end of the meal, you'll question whether you're in New Orleans or Athens. A rallying cry at George's is "Laissez les bons temps rouler."

420 Macon Hwy., 706-548-3359
georgeslowcountrytable.com

TIP
Thursday date night serves up prime rib and wine for two plus. A monthly Scotch dinner provides samplings from multiple vendors while patrons enjoy dinner. Sign up for the newsletter to receive updates

DEVOUR A STEAK CUBANO
AT CALI N TITO'S

Having lunch at Cali N Tito's is like a quick trip to Latin America. And judging by the size of the crowds, it appears everyone in Athens needs a vacation. This unpretentious eatery is a favorite among college students and locals. The portions are huge, and the food, spiced perfectly. The small roadside location with limited seating serves hundreds daily on campus. Palm trees flag both locations. The second location allows for more inside seating, and its party atmosphere is a plus for the kids. Get in line and place your order at the front counter; within minutes, your chips and queso and drinks will be on your table. Every item on the menu is good, but if you do not try the Cuban Sandwich (pork, steak, or chicken), you'll have to make a second trip.

1245 Cedar Shoals Dr., 706-355-7087
1427 S Lumpkin St., 706-227-9979
calintitos.com

TASTE THE WORLD

The Expat
Italian cuisine
1680 S Lumpkin St., 706-521-5041
theexpatathens.com

The Royal Peasant
British & Indian–inspired dishes
1675 S Lumpkin St., 706-549-7920
royalpeasant.com

Shokitini
Japanese cuisine
251 W Clayton St., Ste. 117, 706-353-7933
shokitini.com

Taste of India
Indian cuisine
1040 Gaines School Rd., Ste. 119, 706-559-0000
indiaathens.com

Agua Linda Taqueria
Mexican cuisine
2082 Timothy Rd., 706-543-0154
aqualindarestaurant.com

DePalma's
Italian cuisine
401 E Broad St., 706-354-6966
depalmasitaliancafe.com

el Barrio tacos & tequila
Tacos and more
1331 S Milledge Ave., 706-850-0708
elbarrioathens.com

D92 Korean BBQ
Korean BBQ
1080 Baxter St., 706-850-7990

FEED ON FARMERS' FARE
AT FARM CART

It's a biscuit world in Athens, and Farm Cart is deep in the biscuit battle. From growing vegetables on their farm to selling them at the Athens Farmers Market to running their own food truck, Mike and Iwalani Farfour greet diners on Baxter in their new storefront. All products are locally sourced, and sauces and jams are house-made. Square buttermilk biscuits dress sandwich options for breakfast and lunch. Southern staples like sausage gravy, fruit jams, and fried eggs are held between square packaging; however, Hawaiian buns frame the burgers at lunch. If it's a to-go day, order mimosas to go as well as a dozen of their mini or hefty buttermilk biscuits.

1074 Baxter St., 706-580-8150
thefarmcart.com

FUN FACT

Collective Harvest provides sustainably grown products by small-scale farms to the community. From vegetables to fruit to meat to flowers, shop online and take home a taste of locally grown products.

CHASE A GAME AND DRINK A DARTH ROAST
AT THE ROOK & PAWN
BOARD GAME CAFÉ

One of the first board game cafés in the Southeast, Rook and Pawn began with a love of board games. Put down the phone, talk with friends, and compete in a friendly game of Monopoly—or one of the hundreds of games available. It's all about disconnecting and living in the moment. At first look, it's like an old-London bookshop café with the bar on the right, game shelf on the left. Ask the staff for the perfect game, pay just $5, and you'll have all-day access to every game in the shop. There are also some available at no charge. You can join others in a group game. Want a quiet game while enjoying food and drink? Order food and enter the Victorian-era alleyway into the back part of the café. A small menu of sandwiches and salads are offered with a variety of teas and Jittery Joe's coffees. It's the way gaming was intended to be.

294 W Washington St., Ste. 300, 706-543-5040
therookandpawn.com

FIND UNIQUE CRAFT AND INTERNATIONAL BREWS
AT TRAPPEZE PUB

It's the perfect downtown location to find the unexpected; and for the win, what other restaurant offers boiled peanuts by the cup or bowl? Look for the iconic mint green antique Chevy parked out front. Slide in for a generous pub fare selection plus Belgian and old-world-style beers on tap. In addition, mead from South Carolina and cider from Kennesaw, Georgia, plus sours from across the US, add a little variety to the mix. A favorite is Light IPA from Tantrum Brewing in Cleveland, Georgia. Want more variety? Kölsch German beer, along with Scotch ales and Belgian whites, can make the most passionate beer aficionado drive miles for this selection. A hearty selection of brews is a requisite for washing down pub fare like the famous Belgian fries or the North Carolina trout. Check out Sunday brunch and pair a cocktail with the Belgian waffles or breakfast tacos. Trappeze Pub is the sister venue to South Kitchen + Bar. Recently renovated, the pub is open daily.

269 N Hull St., 707-543-8997
trappezepub.com

BEER AND WINE PULSE

The Pine Bar

Enjoy tapas, oysters, and charcuterie on the patio. A lovely gathering spot in the Five Points neighborhood, the Pine Bar provides a comprehensive list of wines by the glass and bottle, and signature cocktails with small plates for brunch. Reservations are encouraged, especially for the weekend champagne brunch.

1235 S Milledge Ave., 706-395-6278

thepineathens.com

Blind Pig Tavern

A family-friendly spot, Blind Pig Tavern offers relaxation and good food at all of its four locations. Burgers and wings rule, and its Monday through Friday happy hour from 2 p.m. until 7 p.m. serves up brews with a bartender's choice special each day.

312 E Washington St., 706-548-3442

2440 W Broad St., 706-208-7979

2301 College Station, 706-850-4919

22 N Main St., Watkinsville, 706-310-4450

blindpigtavern.com

FEAST ON A SLICE OF BUTTERMILK PIE
FROM THE YESTERDAY CAFÉ

If it's good enough for Carrie Underwood's wedding reception, you can bet it's definitely worth a trip to neighboring Greensboro to give it a try. The pie's reputation put this lovely southern town on the map, only 35 miles from Athens, and dubbed "Home of the Buttermilk Pie." It's located in the line of storefronts in the downtown strip. A market board strategically placed on the sidewalk outside the front door lists the day's specials that might include meatloaf or pork chops. Inside the café, historical photos decorate walls, providing the perfect short read for the meal wait. And, don't let the word *buttermilk* scare you. It puts gold in this confection. Locals will tell you not to leave the café without a slice of buttermilk pie to end the meal. This is what southern tastes like.

114 N Main St., Greensboro, 706-453-0800
theyesterdaycafe.com

TASTE THE FIRST CRAFT BEER IN SPACE
AT OCONEE BREWING COMPANY

If your beer is out of this world, it must be from Oconee Brewing Company. From painting signage on the brewery's building to rigging a payload under the four-pound requirement by the Federal Aviation Administration (FAA), Andrew Henry always dreamed of being the first muralist in space. Brewer Taylor Lamm thought it was an incredible idea, and they built a shell from a Styrofoam cooler to house two GoPro cameras and GPS tracking equipment, and added a bag of hops for good luck, plus a couple of business cards. They duct-taped and secured the payload, and at its end, tucked in a can of Round Here Beer. They added the artwork from Henry, filed a flight plan with the FAA, and the launch went off without a hitch. The balloon made it through the jet stream to around 120,432 feet before the balloon finally burst, making Round Here the first beer in space.

202 N West St., Greensboro, 706-920-1177
oconeebrewingco.com

FUN FACT
Brewmaster Taylor Lamm traded banking for brewing. Located in a 6,000-square-foot former mill warehouse, Oconee Brewing has a full production facility and tasting room. Open Thursday through Saturday.

ORDER (AT LEAST) A HALF DOZEN POTATO DONUTS
AT CAFÉ RACER COFFEE + DONUTS

Leave the city behind for breakfast and point your car toward Crawford. Pay attention. A small, blue, container-type structure sits just off the side of the road, and inside, you'll find the best donuts and breakfast sandwiches outside the Athens city limits. Serving Counter Culture Coffee and big ol' breakfast biscuits through a double drive-through window, smiling people deliver one or a half dozen potato donuts and a biscuit sandwich that will change your life. The biskies (biscuits) are the stars. The Bonjorno borders on over-the-top. Combine jalapeño cream cheese, fried hash browns, house-made pimento cheese, thick-cut bacon, and a fried egg, all topped with Racer Sauce plus lettuce and tomato to up the wow factor. There are 13 more selections if the Bonjorno doesn't do it. There's also tatertacos and breakfast tacos, and lattes and macchiatos.

3 Arnoldsville Rd., Crawford, 706-899-0210
caferacer78.com

THE BEST CARBS EVER

Big City Bread Café

Located inside a former Salvation Army building, Big City creates specialty breads, pastries, and biscuits in their wholesale bakery operation. Have a meal on the large patio underneath the Chinese elm trees or in their interior dining bar. A second location, Little City Diner, is at 135 Cherokee Road, Winterville. Open for breakfast and lunch.
393 N Finley St., #2482, 706-353-0029
bigcitybreadcafe.com

Independent Baking Company

It's a Five Points favorite, producing loaves of bread and delicious pastries. Watch the bakers create world-class breads from four simple ingredients. Find unique breads like kalamata olive, sourdough rye, Danish rye, and whole spelt.
1625 S Lumpkin St., 706-850-3550
independentbaking.com

Zombie Coffee and Donuts

The red eyeball logo illustrates that everyone is a Zombie before morning coffee and donuts. All donuts are made on the spot, allowing customers to create the perfect combination of toppings without any limits or price inflation. Add a cup of fair-trade coffee, made any way you like, and watch the Zombie disappear.
350 E Broad St., 706-850-2526
eatzombiedonuts.com

BE FIRST
AT LAST RESORT GRILL

Their symbol, the Georgia Vidalia onion, draws attention to their southern roots. Much like many local-entrepreneurial eateries, Last Resort Grill highlights the area farmers, from their seasonal produce to trout sourced from North Georgia streams. Their unique southwestern-inspired twist on common ingredients is what drives diners into this downtown establishment over and over. Born a music club in the 1960s with performers like Doc Watson and Jimmy Buffett, this colorful space opens for dinner daily and brunch on the weekends. A small plate start might include crispy pork belly that will lead to big plates like Six Hour Pig. The New Struggleville pasta dish elevates shrimp and pasta ribbons to an entirely different realm. Stop by the mural that covers the exterior wall for a quick photo with the iconic onion.

174–184 W Clayton St., 706-549-0810
lastresortgrill.com

TIP
Famous Cecilia's Cake Shop slices are a must. Cake lovers unite behind this long-standing symbol of Athens, and if one taste is not enough, order an entire cake to go. ceciliascakeshop.com

---

TASTE THE DIFFERENCE
THAT HOME.MADE MAKES

Scratch provides home.made's distinction. Open for dinner, this eatery commits to a memorable dining experience with dishes sourced from the community's farms. Southern signature dishes include deviled eggs, spinach salads, and a southern favorite, tomato pie. Walk next door to Sidecar, where the experience can take a smaller yet unique turn. A Battery Bowl of toffee vanilla wafers and cheese straws gets it started. If these tickle your palate, purchase a bag from the shop to-go.

1072 Baxter St., 706-206-9216
homemadeathens.com

TIP
home.made is closed Sundays and Mondays. Parties of seven or more require reservations.

LEAD OFF
WITH AMUSE-BOUCHE
DURING ATHENS WINE WEEKEND

Four events over the course of a weekend can change one's opinion of wine. The annual Athens Wine Weekend, sponsored by the Classic Center Cultural Foundation, connects wine lovers with new experiences, all while benefiting the arts in Athens. Events begin with an amuse-bouche with a sampling of culinary artistry paired with award-winning wines. The Grand Tasting offers a casual experience to sample wines from around the world, coupled with a little wine education. The Gourmet Dinner is fine dining at its best, with a multicourse meal paired with wines to complement. The Sparkling Wine Brunch is a mimosa and culinary buffet. This event increases the scholarship offerings for students in performing, visual, and culinary arts programs.

300 N Thomas St., 706-208-0900
classiccenter.com

FOLLOW THE FISH
TO MARKER 7 COASTAL GRILL

Located on one of the five corners in the popular Five Points neighborhood, Marker 7 Coastal Grill delivers the coast to Athens. From oysters from the Gulf of Mexico to shrimp from coastal Georgia, dining here satisfies the lust for ocean breezes. It's what you come to expect from your favorite seaside establishment. Platters of crusty coconut shrimp, crunchy cornbread hushpuppies, and shrimp and grits make this a local favorite every night of the week. Local craft beers wash down seafood while signature cocktails like the Moscow mule and the Dark 'N Stormy provide the perfect punctuation to a meal. Parking is tricky and limited, so if you're within walking distance, Milledge Avenue makes for a nice evening stroll. The line forms early for the dinner crowd, so think ahead and arrive early. Everything is first come, first served. Open daily for dinner, with lunch served, Tuesday through Sunday.

1195 S Milledge Ave., 706-850-3451
marker7coastalgrill.com

QUEUE THE PULLED PORK
AT PULASKI HEIGHTS BBQ

Pulaski Heights BBQ is one of those "until the meat sells out" type of places. Slow-cooked meats are their specialty, with pulled pork, St. Louis dry-rub ribs, brisket, and chicken as their stars. Located in the historic Leathers Building in the Pulaski neighborhood, the restaurant entrance faces Chase Street. Outside dining is available as well as a small indoor space. They also offer family dinners and even a Pig Pickin' that feeds up to 12 people. Sounds like a tailgate dream. Vegan, vegetarian, and gluten-free options are available. Sauces cover the South and include Carolina gold mustard and Korean style as well as classic sweet tomato and spicy vinegar. You can also bring your knife for sharpening.

675 Pulaski St., 706-583-9600
pulaskiheightsbbq.com

GET SAUCY

Dawg Gone Good BBQ

It's a hole-in-the-wall, classic downtown location that smokes ribs and barbecue. Outside dining provides a view of the busy downtown. Open Monday through Saturday for lunch and early dinner.
224 W Hancock Ave., 706-613-9799
dawggonegoodbbq.com

Saucehouse

An authentic BBQ joint with a roll of paper towels filling in for napkins. Walk the line and choose the meal, vessels, and sides. Nine sauces are available. Opt for the banana pudding to finish the meal. When it rains, you get a free side. On the bar side, you'll find a full bar with 29 beers on draft.
830 W Broad St., 706-363-3351
saucehouse.com

SELECT THE EXTRAORDINARY
AT SHIRAZ FINE WINE & GOURMET

From the floor to the ceiling, wine bottles from every part of the world balance on curved wooden racks. Having one of the most extensive wine selections in the city, Shiraz Fine Wine & Gourmet offers a glass of wine as you examine the national and international selections, never the same twice. Wines are chosen by owner and sommelier Emily Garrison, and there's not a single one she hasn't tasted. Noted as Best of Georgia for its wine selection, Shiraz showcases gifts of wine and wine-related merchandise as well as items for the cook and home. Cheese plates are available on Fridays. On the first Saturday of each month, there's a guided wine tasting every 20 minutes. However, it's the wine club that dazzles with personal selections and discounts. The newsletters are chock-full of recipes to enhance the wine.

678 Pulaski St., Ste. 400, 706-208-0010
shirazathens.com

GET YOUR STRIPES (AND THE PIMENTO CHEESE BURGER)
AT WHITE TIGER GOURMET

It's the best greeting in Athens: the smell of pecan-wood-smoked BBQ. Take a seat at the picnic tables at this neighborhood eatery, where everything comes wrapped in signature red and white checkered paper. Located in the historic Boulevard District, White Tiger Gourmet lives in a 100-year-old structure that was originally a grocery store and served the mill neighborhood. Open the screen door, and it feels like you've stepped back to a time when customers were served at the wooden counter immediately upon arrival. On the walls, works by local artists decorate and welcome. The aroma of BBQ persuades you to order some version, whether on a plate or a sandwich, but local favorites like burgers, salads, and mac 'n' cheese make the choosing difficult. With its affordable pricing, choose everything. When warm weather is in season, the picnic tables out front are filled, while the limited seating inside is for those looking to escape the Georgia heat. Open Tuesday through Sunday for lunch and dinner, the white tiger waits for you at the front counter. White Tiger is always BYOB.

217 Hiawassee Ave., 706-353-6847
whitetigergourmet.com

MUSIC
AND ENTERTAINMENT

DISCOVER THE ARTIST INSIDE
AT ARTINI'S ART LOUNGE

Can't paint? According to the painters at Artini's, "If you can dip a brush into paint, you can be an artist." Who knew? Dive right in and share the class with 30 new friends and an instructor/artist who will prove imperfection can be beautiful and fun. For the difficult shapes, they'll stencil them in for you. To protect your fashion, they'll provide an apron. To make it less intimidating, they'll top off the plastic wine glass. Everything you need, they provide. What's not to love? Northern Lights. Flower Flow. Abstract Arch. The instructors have tons of design options, so uncovering your inner artist will be as easy as choosing what you love.

337 Prince Ave., 706-353-8530
artinisartlounge.com

TIP
Visit the website and choose the Class Calendar. Although walk-ins are welcome, reservations are recommended.

FLASH THE LIGHTS
AT FLICKER THEATRE AND BAR

Welcome to your downtown living room. Take a seat at the bar, order your favorite cocktail, and soon, the evening's entertainment will set this intimate space on fire. Featuring karaoke and comedy shows plus local bands, there's something going on most nights of the week. Unique to this venue is the Flicker Film Society, a collective of film-loving Athenians who host films each month at the theater. If you love cult, gore, erotica, or just plain weird movies, you'll want to check out the calendar for showings. Inspiring cocktails like the Jolene, a nod to Dolly Parton, and even Irish coffee and the usual favorites and craft beers go perfectly with their legendary Pouch Pies. Check their full calendar, available online, for upcoming music acts, comedy shows, and weird movies.

263 W Washington St., 706-546-0039
flickertheatreandbar.com

PROVE THE POWER OF A SINGLE LIGHT
AT 40 WATT

Once upon a time, the club, lit by a single 40-watt light bulb, was located in the College Street apartment of a Pylon band member. This small space rocked with underground events and raucous parties, which heralded a need for a larger space. Fast-forward decades to 1991, when R.E.M. played an acoustic set to promote its new album, *Out of Time.* Up-and-coming acts make it a point to headline 40 Watt. At its sixth location, 40 Watt forges music gold. At the midpoint of its biography, local legends B-52s, Drive-By Truckers, Widespread Panic, and R.E.M. headlined, as well as Nirvana, the Black Crowes, Kings of Leon, Kenny Chesney, and others. From punk to pop to county to rap, the 40 Watt stage proved the power of one stage to launch a career.

285 W Washington St., 706-549-7871
40watt.com

CATCH A RISING STAR
AT GEORGIA THEATRE

This space introduces stars. Notice the pattern in Athens? They care for their own and do everything in their power to catapult each to stardom. Local artists like Florida Georgia Line played here prior to their Grammy nomination. The Red Hot Chili Peppers, Neil Young, Billy Joel, Dire Straits, and Eric Clapton have played here as well. Built in 1889, it was first a YMCA, then a hotel, Masonic temple, Sears store, Methodist church, and, finally, in 1935, a theater called Georgia Theatre. Fire consumed it in 2009, and the community rallied to restore it as the city's premier live-music venue. Most shows are standing room only, so if seating is required, make arrangements with the venue pre-show. Limited barstools are available on a first-come, first-served basis. A rooftop bar offers an amazing view of the city plus a full food and drink menu.

215 N Lumpkin St., 706-850-7670
georgiatheatre.com

TIP
No matter if you've visited a hundred times, a photo in front of the Broadway-style marquee sign is a must.

DANCE IN THE STREETS
AT ATHFEST MUSIC
AND ARTS FESTIVAL

What's better than a free street party? Thousands converge into historic downtown during this highly anticipated, three-day summer event to celebrate the creative pulse and rich music history of Athens. Local musicians, artisans, and performers take over outdoor stages for the largest block party of the season. It's a family affair with KidsFest, featuring performances by and for young people and activities that are pure fun. There's also a market, multiple beer gardens, and local eateries, plus retail vendors. Other activities include a Club Crawl plus other VIP experiences. Since its inception in 1997, the festival has continued to raise money for AthFest Educates, a nonprofit that funds high-quality music and arts education for local K–12 youth.

Washington Street between Pulaski and Lumpkin streets, 706-548-1973
athfest.com

GRAB A SEAT AND SIT A SPELL
AT PORCHFEST

Offer 100 porches to 100 musicians, and you get a PorchFest. From afternoon into early evening, six historic neighborhoods host musicians on the front porches of homes, drawing thousands for a day of walking from one house to another. Each hour is filled with at least 20 concerts. Sponsored by the nonprofit Historic Athens, preservation of the history and heritage of the city drives this event. Many of the neighborhoods and historic buildings escape visitors' eyes, and drawing on its musical backdrop, this event showcases the districts that are the foundation of the Classic City and those who have supported the independent art scene. Grab some merch while you're there, and support the city's music legacy and the new talent beginning to take the stage.

Boulevard, Buena Vista, Cobbham, Newtown, Normaltown,
and Pulaski Heights neighborhoods
historicathens.com

PARADE TWO BLOCKS WITH 10 GREATS
ON THE ATHENS MUSIC WALK OF FAME

For decades, Athens has produced some of the greatest acts in music history. This rich heritage attracts fans from around the world to make a pilgrimage to Athens to see where it all began. It's a two-square-block area in downtown that includes music venues that played significant roles in the rise of the first 10 inductees. Inductees were chosen based on their contributions to Athens, careers, diversity, musical styles, and historical context. From North Lumpkin to Pulaski, look for a series of bronze sidewalk plaques with gold inscriptions honoring the performers. They are strategically placed in areas that played a vital role in their rise to fame. As an ongoing project, additional artists will be added.

Athens Music Hall of Fame Inductees
B-52s
Danger Mouse
Drive-By Truckers
The Elephant 6 Recording Company
Hall Johnson
Neal Pattman
Pylon
R.E.M.
Vic Chesnutt
Widespread Panic

PARTY IN COSTUME
AT WILD RUMPUS

It's a Mardi Gras–flavored Halloween celebration! Make noise, take to the streets in costume, and parade downtown at the Rumpus Rally. At the end, enjoy the massive dance party with rousing music and acrobatic aerialists. Each year, the sponsors of the event earmark a beneficiary for the proceeds. Although it's an October bash, Rumpus, along with their sponsors, gives back all year long to local organizations in need of financial assistance and mentorship.

Downtown Athens
wildrumpus.org

RESURRECT THE DEEP SOUTH
AT WILDWOOD REVIVAL

It's adult summer camp set to a great soundtrack. Raising the bar on the music festivals, Wildwood Revival takes over historic Cloverleaf Farm just outside Athens to create a true experience. Playing off Athens's storied music scene, the creators of Wildwood built the festival on curiosity and enthusiasm for music. Every genre of music contributes to the itinerary: country, blues, gospel, soul, jazz, rock 'n' roll. There's an artisan market with vintage clothing, antiques, woodworkers, tintype photography, leather markers, and handmade crafts. What's old is new again. The entire experience includes a glamping village, Bloody Marys and yoga, and a bluegrass brunch, as well as foods from seasonal offerings coupled with the best coffee around. The intimate environment serves as the perfect setting for late-night picking sessions around the campfire as storytellers set stories to music. Meet under the pecan trees for this three-day awakening.

Cloverleaf Farm
536 Wolfskin Rd., Arnoldsville
wildwoodrevival.com

CATCH
THE LATEST RELEASE
AT CINÉ

Within its historic walls is the best of all worlds. As the only independent art house movie theater in Athens, Ciné plays a vital role in the cultural life of the city. Inspirational and educational film and art exhibits are paramount to its mission. The moviegoing experience is enriched by the art that fills the space. Those who enjoy good cinema, great art, and a good drink are welcome. As a nonprofit organization, Ciné celebrates the diversity of the community, and selections of art and film are made based on enriching the cultural landscape. The schedule of screenings can be found on the website. These include the director's selections as well as Oscar-nominated shorts and full-length features.

234 W Hancock Ave., 706-353-3343
athenscine.com

STRETCH THE CULTURAL FABRIC
AT THE UGA PERFORMING ARTS CENTER

Although not old by the city's standards, the University of Georgia Performing Arts Center is making history in the Classic City. The largest concert hall is the Hugh Hodgson Concert Hall with festival-style seating, and the smaller Ramsey Concert Hall offers intimate seating for recitals and concerts. From national and international solo artists to the familiar Atlanta Symphony Orchestra, talent graces the stages and brings world-class performers to Athens. What might not otherwise be accessible to this community, the UGA Performing Arts Center makes possible. The Performing Arts Center records many of its concerts for national broadcasts on American Public Media's *Performance Today*. Visit the website to view the available seasonal archives.

230 River Rd., 706-542-4400
pac.uga.edu

TAKE IN
A BROADWAY SHOW
AT THE CLASSIC CENTER

No matter what entertains you, find it at the Classic Center. "Be Impressed" with everything inside this venue. From Broadway plays to Grammy-award-winning artists to the funniest man on Earth, the Classic Center is the center of North Georgia's performing arts cosmos. It hosts more than 1,200 events each year, and, being rooted in the community, many events are devoted to outreach and opportunity for children and adults. Its Broadway Series is a popular event and hosts some of the most popular productions on the Great White Way. Check the schedule before you visit the city, and plan an extraordinary night out at the lively venue.

300 N Thomas St., 706-208-0900
classiccenter.com

FLIP THROUGH VINYL
AT WUXTRY RECORDS

It's the last remaining vinyl store in Athens. Since 1976, people have been flipping through the records at Wuxtry Records, simply watching the cover art roll until they find the one that moves their soul. Find new as well as gently used LPs and 45s of some of the greatest music of this era. This Athens location is where singer-songwriter Michael Stipe met guitarist Peter Buck, the team that would later become the rock band R.E.M.

197 E Clayton St., 706-369-9428
wuxtryrecords.com

REVEL
IN THE LATE-NIGHT
AGENDA DOWNTOWN

It's no secret that Athens is a party town. For every college student, local and visitor, there's a nightspot created uniquely for them. From the hole-in-the-walls in downtown to the large-event venues scattered throughout the county, Athens provides a hub for the classic venues as well as those that are out of this world.

Sister Louisa's Church of the Living Room and Ping Pong Emporium
Live music and drinks, LGBTQ
254 W Clayton St., 706-850-3668
sisterlouisaschurch.com

The World Famous
Late-night hangout with live music, eats, and brews
351 N Hull St., 706-543-4002

Hi Lo Lounge
Bar and lounge serving drinks and
three-way chili
1354 Prince Ave., 706-850-8561
hiloathens.com

Nowhere Bar
A local dive for pool, beer,
and live music
240 N Lumpkin St.
nowherebarlive.com

The Warehouse
Live music venue
346 E Broad St.
thewarehouseathens.com

Wonderbar
Eat, drink, and play video games
240 E Washington St.

LIVE ON ISLAND TIME
AT ALLGOOD LOUNGE

It's all about the rooftop patio, soaking up the sun, and taking in whatever happens to be on the big-screen TV. With a cocktail from the Tiki bar, no matter what is going on around you, it's all good. It's three vertical floors jam-packed with a full service bar, pool tables, big-screen TVs, and an outdoor tiki bar perfect for the warm summer days in Athens. It's a build-your-own Bloody Mary bar every day of the week. Signature cocktails take you on a journey with the Georgia Peach, the Irish mule, and the Brazillan Breeze. On game days, students and fans fill all three floors celebrating and watching post-game coverage on the big screens.

256 E Clayton St., 706-549-0166
allgoodlounge.com

FUSE THE OLD AND NEW
AT THE FOUNDRY

It's the warmth of the vintage wooden bar and the exposed brick that make it inviting. At the Foundry, the oldest building on the Graduate Athens property, friends meet for a round at the bar or listen to live music in its three-tiered audience space. It provides an intimate audience experience and is one of the favorite places for events. The Graduate Athens welcomes out-of-town guests to inviting traditional rooms, but they also have the historic Hoyt House, a 19th-century farmhouse, available for stays. Within walking distance of downtown, it's a place to lay your head and a corner for entertainment and drinks.

295 Dougherty St., 706-549-7020
graduatehotels.com

SPORTS
AND RECREATION

TAILGATE
AT A UGA HOME FOOTBALL GAME

The influx of RVs into Athens ramps up long before game day. Once in place and unloaded, a sea of red fills the designated tailgating spaces. While stadium gates open at noon on Saturday, the celebration of the impending game happens before then. At the crack of dawn, grills fire up and coolers open wide as the Bulldog faithful take over the campus. It's not only your presence at a game that is important, but also what you wear and eat while prepping for the day's festivities. According to a local culinary expert, starting with a Bloody Mary ensures victory. Follow with Brunswick stew, pulled pork BBQ, baby back ribs, coleslaw, bread pudding, and of course, iced tea and champagne. All that remains is waiting for the Dawgs to head between the hedges.

TIPS

Looking for perfect tailgate fixins? A local favorite is Stripling's General Store on Highway 316. Stop on your way into Athens for fresh quality meats and sides made from scratch—that is, if you can get in the parking lot. striplings.com

TOP TAILGATE SPOTS
On Campus
Central Campus at Legion Field
with reserved parking and tailgate services

Intramural Fields

Myers Quad
(home of ESPN *College GameDay* or *SEC Nation*)

North Campus and Herty Field

Bulldog Tailgate Club
Turnkey tailgate packages
bulldogtailgateclub.com

Off Campus
The Classic Center
Multiple tailgate packages with 24-hour security
classiccenter.com

TailGAte Station
Luxury tailgate facility with space ownership
tailgatestation.net

RACE LIKE AN ATHENIAN
IN THE ATHHALF 5K/HALF-MARATHON

There's more than one way to see the city. Runners hit their stride through the downtown streets, the historic neighborhoods of Boulevard, Normaltown, and Cobbham, leading to the UGA campus. Thousands line the streets, cheering them on as they make their way through the finish line. In conjunction with AthFest, the added running element was kicked into high gear by the people involved with AthFest Educates, a nonprofit that funds music and arts education for local K–12 youth. A USA Track and Field–certified course and sanctioned event, runners return year after year to run the course. There is a four-hour time limit for the half-marathon and a one-hour limit for all 5k runners. Runners, ages 14 and up, are eligible. Rain or shine, the race takes place during the fall. Can't make the trip to Athens? There's a virtual option, too.

Starting line: The Classic Center
Finish line: Sanford Stadium, 706-548-1973
athhalf.com

SCREAM
FOR THE HOME TEAM

Athens is a sports lover's wonderland. Any sport is as close as your fingertips! All UGA sports ticketing takes place online at the official website; create a personal account, so everything is in place and secure. Tickets are also available through StubHub. If you're eyeing a specific team and date, buy tickets early. If it's a football ticket you seek, buy yesterday. All Georgia Bulldog tickets are digital; no physical tickets are issued.

M=Men's; W=Women's

Fall Sports
Football
Soccer W
Volleyball
Cross Country M/W
Track and Field M/W

Winter Sports
Basketball M/W
Equestrian W
Tennis M/W
Gymnastics W
Ice Hockey

Spring Sports
Baseball
Softball
Golf M/W
Georgia Swim and Dive M/W

georgiadogs.com

LACE UP
FOR ATHENS ON ICE

During January, the Classic Center transforms the Akins Ford Arena into an ice pallet for public ice skating. The myth that Southerners can't maneuver on the ice is just that, a myth. Admission includes the bright orange ice skates, and if you're making it a family affair for 10 or more, there's a discount. If you're not skating, you're welcome to come watch others take to the ice. Season passes are also available. The Classic Center ticketing is now digital, so there are no issues with paper passes. Simply pull up the website, choose the perfect time, and purchase a ticket for public skating. Weekend adult public skate is open for ages 18 and up. Tuesdays are open for adult hockey drop-in. Check the website for schedules. Public ice skating takes place from November through the first of February, when the Ice Dawgs take over the ice.

300 N Thomas St., 706-208-0900
classiccenter.com

GET BACK TO NATURE
AT SANDY CREEK NATURE CENTER

For decades, people have ventured just outside the city limits for a respite at the 225-acre Sandy Creek Nature Center. Privately owned, Sandy Creek Nature Center is an educational facility plus a getaway for swimming, horseback riding, biking, and many other outdoor activities. There's an 1815-vintage log house near the visitor's center. The center is filled with exhibits of live animals and water creatures and offers educational programs, plus fishing classes and other outdoor adventures. Four miles of trails are open to visitors. The variety of flora and fauna, plus little creatures scurrying through the woodlands, bring the world of nature close. In the spring, take in the Tadpole one-mile run or the Frog Hop 5K, depending on age. In the fall, run the Jack-O'-Lantern Joy 5K or Goblin one-mile fun run.

205 Old Commerce Rd., 706-610-3615
accgov.com/sandycreeknaturecenter

FOLLOW THE RIVER
ON THE NORTH
OCONEE RIVER GREENWAY

Green drives the trails that cover three and a half miles of natural surface and eight miles of concrete that ushers foot traffic out of the city. Constantly evolving and growing, this trail system supports pedestrians and cyclists. Parking is available at Dudley Park at the southern terminus and Sandy Creek Nature Center at the northern terminus of the trail. Open from sunrise to sunset, the popular greenway is the perfect walk for everyone.

Oconee Rivers Greenway
706-613-3615
accgov.com

SEE THE CITY ON FOOT

North Oconee River Trail
Runs from Sandy Creek Nature Center to Bailey Street
Multi-use, paved trail for pedestrians and bicyclists

East Campus Connector
Runs from the east side of Athens to the UGA campus
Multi-use, concrete trail for pedestrians and bicyclists

Cook's Trail
Trailheads at Sandy Creek Nature Center
and Sandy Creek Park
4.1-mile natural surface trail open to foot traffic only
Trail does not loop and may flood during heavy rain

Trail Creek Trail
Located within Virginia Walker Park
1-mile trail links parks to neighborhoods
Multi-use, paved trail for pedestrians and bicyclists

Pulaski Heights Trail
Trail connects Pulaski Street to Hull and Hoyt streets
Multi-use, one-quarter-mile paved trail for
pedestrians and bicyclists

Milledge Extension Trail
Trail connects Milledge Ave. to South Milledge Ave.
Multi-use, one-quarter-mile paved trail for
pedestrians and bicyclists

RACE ON TWO WHEELS
AT TWILIGHT CRITERIUM

Take to the streets at the premier professional men's and women's racing event in Georgia, the Twilight Criterium. And it is just like Athens to build a festival around a singular event. Music, food, and vendors frame this international event. The Twilight Criterium attracts cyclists and teams from all over the globe. The amateur racing begins early on a Saturday on the main course downtown, and qualifiers continue on to the main event that night. The .59-mile course has a 10-foot elevation gain and takes over Washington and Hancock streets. Women compete first, followed by the men. Along with the cyclists' competition, there's a Twilight 5K requiring registration. A kid's 1K fun run is free but requires pre-registration.

Downtown Athens
athenstwilight.com

RIDE THE RAILS ALONG THE GEORGIA RAILROAD CORRIDOR
ON THE FIREFLY TRAIL

A planned 39-mile rail-trail that will run from Athens to Union Point is partially open. The trail runs along the historic Athens branch of the Georgia Railroad corridor. Each year, the Firefly Trail Ticket to Ride event welcomes cyclists to ride the roads that connect Athens to Union Point. Proceeds from the ride help generate momentum toward completing the project, as well as toward maintaining the trail. The ride can be up to 87 miles, offering riders options to tailor their ride to fit their style. Since this trail is mainly on flat land, it can be enjoyed by everyone, regardless of age or physical ability. The Firefly Trail Race Series includes a year-long series of rides in Winterville, Maxeys, Crawford, and Union Point. A virtual option is also available.

fireflytrail.com

STRUT THE DAWG WALK
WITH THE FOOTBALL PLAYERS AND DAWG NATION INTO SANFORD STADIUM ON GAME DAY

Get in line and hold your breath. The Redcoat Band's once-upon-a-time pregame warmup exercise activity morphed into one of the most coveted traditions on campus. The Dawg Walk happens, like clockwork, two hours and 15 minutes before the start of every home game in the Tate Center parking lot. The players step off the buses that line Lumpkin Street and head toward Gate 1. Playing "Glory, Glory," the Redcoat Band takes the lead as athletes and coaches head into the stadium. Thousands of fans line the lot, high-fiving and screaming. It's not for the faint of heart. Even if you don't have a ticket for the game, you can get in on game-day excitement. No ticket needed for the Dawg Walk. Get in line early and don't forget to wear red and black.

45 Baxter St.

FLY WITH EASE
AT CANOPY STUDIO

Did you know there is a community of believers in the art of flying dance trapeze and the health and well-being benefits that come from moving upside-down on ropes? At Canopy Studio, the movement arts are a thing of beauty, and the community has embraced its classes and performances. It offers trapeze, fabrics, acrobatics, conditioning, and flexibility classes, and all ages and abilities are welcome. Designed for children and adults, the programs start low and work on individual tricks and form, building strength. It even offers a class for those over 53, proving age is not a barrier. Workshops and private classes are available, and registration is open on the website. Spending more than a weekend in the Classic City? This is the perfect act to build your visit around.

160-6 Tracy St., 706-549-8501
canopystudio.org

TOSS A FOOTBALL
ON HERTY FIELD

Abraham Baldwin was the first UGA president. The first mascot was a goat, and Herty Field was the original home field. The first game ever played was against Mercer, which ended with a shutout for Georgia, 50–0. The final score is a bit of a mystery, since the official scorer missed at least one touchdown because he walked to Broad Street to purchase a bottle of whiskey during the game. The second game, a 0–10 loss to Auburn, initiated what is now known as "the Deep South's Oldest Rivalry." It wasn't until the 1920s that the university officially claimed the Bulldog as its mascot. Herty Field, located on North Campus and known as Alumni Athletic Field, is a green space that alumni visit every time they return to campus.

FUN FACT

The iconic scoreboard that stood at the east end of Sanford Stadium through the 1978 season belongs to an Athens fan intent on preserving this piece of Georgia football history.

MANEUVER THE CORN MAZE
AT WASHINGTON FARMS

It just wouldn't be spring, or fall, for that matter, without a visit to Washington Farms. For decades, Washington Farms has welcomed families from all over Georgia to their spot this side of heaven for the spring berries and the fall harvest. Spring ramps up with the biggest strawberries you've ever seen, and if you can pick your own without sampling a berry, you're a champ. Pick your own, or call and order ahead of time and they will do the heavy lifting. Don't forget to cool down after berry picking with the best strawberry ice cream on the planet. Fall comes alive with the pumpkin patch and the corn maze, where kids and adults can get lost in a field of imagination. Family fun begins at Washington Farms with the petting zoo, cow train, ball zone, and more activities than you can imagine for an afternoon's worth of fun.

5691 Hog Mountain Rd., Bogart, 706-769-0627
washingtonfarms.net

CHUCK AN AXE AND CHUG A BEER
AT LUMBERJAXE

The beer is optional, but the fun is required. It's a team-bonding, axe-throwing, thrill-seeking kind of place. At Lumberjaxe, it's all about the fun and having an experience that will never be forgotten, and it's the only axe-throwing venue in Athens. Two UGA alumni decided to open an axe-throwing bar, and they wanted to drink beer while throwing. Crazier pursuits have popped up from UGA students, but soon they opened and were the first to be located in a college town. It's fun, and the thrill is most definitely unexpected. Before you take the axe, instructions are given so it's not a blind throw. Anyone over the age of 10 can participate, and everyone must sign a liability waver. Make sure you wear closed-toed shoes. First come, first served. It's usually crowded, so call ahead and reserve a lane. Snacks and local brews are available for purchase.

510 N Lumpkin St., 706-995-7405
lumberjaxe.com

GO TRIPPIN'
ON THE OCONEE RIVER

It's always good to get out on the water, and in Athens the Oconee River provides the perfect cool escape as the temperatures rise in Georgia. Years ago, the Oconee River served as the national boundary waters between the American frontier and the Creek Indian Confederacy. Today, various mill ruins stand like ghosts along the river. Oconee Joe, historian, naturalist, and conservationist, has become the premier river guide for an eco/history trip along the Oconee River Watershed. The company offers half-day, full-day and multi-day kayak and canoe trips focusing on the region's diverse piedmont ecology and rich human history. Mixing over 70 miles of river sections and 100 miles of cross-country hiking, tours can be packaged to cater to the outdoor adventurer. There's no sandwiches on this trip. After a full day's paddle, enjoy a local charcuterie board served alongside local, seasonal beers around a bonfire. It will be a good day with the man called Oconee Joe.

1350 Old Barnett Shoals Rd.
oconeejoe.com, oldbarnettshoals.com

SPEND TIME IN THE WOODS
AT CITY PARKS

With more than 2,000 acres designated for parks, the city provides everything from arts centers to athletic fields to nature trails within the park system. One of the most popular parks is Memorial Park, located in the Five Points District, which contains the Bear Hollow Zoo, home to non-releasable animals. With unrecoverable injuries or other physical or behavioral issues, the animals lead a normal and protective life while educating the community on their particular variety. There's a wildlife trail home to black bears, bobcats, deer, owls and other wild animals. Most visitors will tell you that the black bear is its biggest star.

Most parks are open from sunrise to sunset. Visit the website for updated hours.

CHOOSE A PARK

Bear Hollow Zoo at Memorial Park
293 Gran Ellen Dr., 706-613-3580

Ben Burton Park
615 Mitchell Bridge Rd.

Bishop Park
708 Sunset Dr.

Dudley Park
100 Dudley Park Dr.

accgov.com

WELCOME
THE HORSEPLAY
AT SOUTHERN CROSS GUEST RANCH

It's not typical by a long stretch. Escape to Southern Cross Guest Ranch for an all-inclusive guest experience that includes no stress, no planning, and no clocks. This small, upscale bed and breakfast takes the roughing it out of the ranch experience. Providing a horseback-riding vacation in a peaceful setting sets this ranch apart from others. You can kick back and lounge, move on the bikes, or explore Madison. The ranch offers a hands-on horseback-riding program, suitable for all levels. With many paint and quarter horses, you'll find a horse that suits your experience level. Choose from a bed-and-breakfast stay, an all-inclusive that includes riding, or an all-inclusive that does not include riding. It's your choice. It's your vacation.

1670 Bethany Church Rd., Madison, 706-342-8027
southcross.com

STEP INTO THE FOREST
ON HUNDRED ACRE FARM

Just outside of the small community of Madison, some 30 miles from Athens, is the Hundred Acre Farm, where a peaceful country retreat is waiting. Its bed and breakfast, the Farmhouse Inn, provides a respite for visitors to make their own schedules or do nothing at all. The beauty of the land compels most visits, as does the therapy it provides. It's the only certified Forest Therapy Trail in the US that supports healing in nature. Through immersion in the forest, or "forest bathing" as it is called in Japan, health benefits are said to multiply, especially in the cardio and immune systems. The walk also is credited with stabilizing mood and improving cognition. A low-intensity activity, the walk progresses slowly. Reservations are required for the trail walks, and fees are waived for guests staying at the Farmhouse Inn. The Introduction to Forest Therapy Walk and the Deep Immersion Forest Walk are both guided walks. A self-guided walk is also available.

1051 Meadow Ln., Madison, 706-342-7933
thefarmhouseinn.com

Double-Barrelled Canon

CULTURE AND HISTORY

RELIVE SEC HISTORY
AT BUTTS–MEHRE HERITAGE HALL AND SPORTS MUSEUM

Named for two previous coaches, Butts–Mehre Heritage Hall is the center of the Bulldog universe. The building houses the players' headquarters and the administrative offices of the Athletic Association. It tells the story of Georgia sports history and UGA favorites. Come see Herschel Walker's Heisman Trophy, as well as the 1980 National Championship trophy. Both men's and women's sports are highlighted in this museum. Don't miss the Vince Dooley Sculpture Garden, which contains 11 garden areas and is about the length of a football field. Vince Dooley led the 1980 Bulldogs to a national championship, and the field between the hedges in Sanford Stadium now holds his name, Dooley Field. The museum is open Monday through Friday during business hours, and admission is free.

1 Selig Cir., 706-542-9036
georgiadogs.com

BRUSH UP
ON THE MURALS OF ATHENS

Creativity, like music and food, pushes Athens forward. The murals that now cover brick walls tell the story of the community while increasing appreciation for the expertise of the artisan. From abstract to graffiti, these murals become part of the city's history. With 29 and counting, the murals of Athens begin in downtown and cover most communities. Each has its own story and design. Find murals in these neighborhoods: Broad Street, Normaltown, Baxter Street, Five Points, Milledge Avenue, and Winterville. A crowd favorite is on the side of Last Resort Grill. Artist David Hale painted *Hope* on the side of retail store Epiphany during the COVID-19 pandemic. A mural created as a tribute to the history of African American entrepreneurship, *Hot Corner: An Athens Legacy*, features Monroe Bowers "Pink" Morton, former owner of the Morton Theatre.

visitathensga.com

TIP
Discover the not-so-obvious mural on the wall of a conference room in UGA's psychology building. Titled *The World at Large*, it depicts those connected with the humanities and arts.

COUNT
THE DAWG STATUES

Who let the Dawgs out? That would be the Athens-Oconee Women's Club in 2003, when they first installed these bulldog beasts around town. It was a small fundraiser by the club to raise money for AIDS relief in Athens. Taking inspiration from other cities that entertained such projects, creator Linda Ford had no idea it would start a movement that has continued for nearly two decades. Each is made of fiberglass and stands four feet in height. Their goal of making art accessible to all residents has transformed the streets of Athens into a smorgasbord of colorful Dawgs, all painted by local artists. Begin your search across from Creature Comforts Brewing and see the "Welcome to Athens" dawg. There are 37 statues around the city, and it's a fun adventure to discover them all.

visitathensga.com

BOOK A TOUR
AND DISCOVER THE HISTORY OF ATHENS

Request shuttle service or book a private tour guide: the Historic Athens tours that depart from the Athens Historic Welcome Center share with you the important districts and locales in the city. The shuttle tour provides an overview of the pre–Civil War homes, historic neighborhoods, downtown, the UGA campus, and other historic districts. Book these tours online on the website. Self-guided tours can be downloaded from the website and include the Milledge Avenue tour, home to many sorority and fraternity chapter houses; Civil War tours focusing on the role Athens played during the conflict; and a UGA campus driving tour.

480 E Dougherty St., 706-353-1820
athenswelcomecenter.com

TIP
The Athens PodTour is downloadable and takes you on a self-guided tour of Athens that includes the Lyndon House Arts Center and the 40 Watt Club.

RING THE CHAPEL BELL
ON NORTH CAMPUS
AFTER A BULLDOGS WIN

After a Bulldogs win, the ringing of the chapel bell can be heard all over the city. It's tradition, and alumni and students stand in line for the chance to jump for the rope and tug for the chime. The bronze bell once housed in the chapel, which was built in 1832, signaled the end of classes, any emergency, or the beginning of religious services. Now located behind the chapel, it is housed in a wooden tower. Today, its sole purpose is to declare a Bulldogs victory between the hedges. And it proves to be a touchstone for visitors, because no one can pass the bell without a pull. Even if it's not a football Saturday in Athens, don't miss the chance to ring the bell to proclaim your visit to the Classic City.

109 Herty Dr.

STAND TALL
WITH THE IRON HORSE

In 1953, a two-toned piece of abstract art in the shape of a horse was erected in front of Reed Hall on campus. Within hours of its installation, students began to vandalize the artwork before setting a fire beneath it. The statue was moved into hiding the next morning. In 1959, L. C. Curtis, a horticulture professor at UGA, moved the sculpture to his farm in Greene County, about 20 miles from the city. It was placed in a field with its rear end facing Athens, a testament to how it felt about the school's betrayal. In 2011, UGA purchased the Curtis Farm for agricultural research and renamed it the Iron Horse Plant Sciences Farm. When driving toward Greensboro, look to the left, and in the middle of a field stands the horse. Visitors would park alongside the highway and, at times, would present a hazard. Soon, a small parking area was carved out of the field to accommodate multiple vehicles making the horse experience a safe one. The location is just over the Greene County line at mile marker 27.

Hwy. 15 N, Greensboro

PICTURE INSPIRATION
AT THE GEORGIA MUSEUM OF ART

Both an academic museum and the official art museum of the state of Georgia, the Georgia Museum of Art displays permanent collections as well as traveling exhibitions. Permanent collections include American paintings of the 19th and 20th centuries as well as European and Asian works and growing collections of southern decorative arts. There are nearly 17,000 items in the permanent collection. Its contemporary footprint has come a long way from its original home in the basement of the library on North Campus. The 20th-century American Art Collection features works by Georgia O'Keeffe, Andrew Wyeth, as well as other influential painters. Galleries are open every day except Monday. Plan your visit by visiting the website and a searchable database that provides images of the works in a collection.

90 Carlton St., 706-542-4662
georgiamuseum.org

PLAY LIKE A CHILD
AT THE STATE BOTANICAL GARDEN OF GEORGIA

Be amazed at one of the most beautiful places in Athens, the State Botanical Garden of Georgia. With education at the heart of its mission, the garden is an extension of the University of Georgia and seeks to nurture and stimulate thinking. Over 313 acres in area, the garden is a place of tranquility and beauty. Trails and nature areas, flora gardens, an international garden, and a hummingbird trail all lead to the Heritage Garden with a collection of heirloom flowers, row crops, and native species. Spring is the most spectacular season with azaleas, dogwoods, and magnolias in full bloom. Just as magnificent is the Alice H. Richards Children's Garden, the garden's newest environment, which creates a sense of place by incorporating native plants and gardens. A canopy walk, multiple observation decks, and a theater provide interactive elements. Make a point to visit the gardens; they're open daily.

2450 S Milledge Ave., 706-542-1244
botgarden.uga.edu

SING ALONG
ON THE MUSIC HISTORY
WALKING TOUR

Don't visit Athens without walking in the footsteps of the music greats. Walk the hall-of-fame trail and then find out what inspired them. The guided music history tour is available with pre-registration for groups of five or more. Want a specialized tour based on specific sights to see? That's available, too. Did you know that the Last Resort Grill began as a music club and bar? That the Coffee Club was raided by the police as R.E.M. played their second show? Before the B-52s could play the Georgia Theatre, they had to pre-sell $1,500 in advance tickets. And this is just scratching the surface of music history. With almost 30 points of interest, the tour will have you reliving your youngers days of rock and roll.

Classic City Tours
706-353-1820
athenswelcomecenter.com

SEE THE FIRST AND ONLY
DOUBLE-BARRELED CANNON

This experimental weapon during the Civil War era didn't quite make the cut. Considered a massive failure, it never saw the throes of a battlefield. Athens-resident John Gilleland designed and built the canon in 1862 when the community suspected an attack from the northern troops. He presented it to the Confederate forces. Fortunately, they turned it down. Gilleland's three experimental firings and uncontrollable balls knocked down a stand of trees, tore up a cornfield, killed a cow, and knocked down a chimney. None of the shots landed near the intended target. It is strategically placed in front of Athens City Hall, pointing toward the enemy North. It's one of the most iconic relics on display in a public area. It is listed in *Ripley's Believe It or Not.*

Grounds of City Hall
301 College Ave.

ROAM
THROUGH THE HISTORICAL HOMES

Antebellum homes define Athens's role in the history of Georgia. The craftsmanship of these beautiful structures serves as a remembrance of the strength of the city. With 16 historic districts plus multiple homes within these districts etched on the National Register of Historic Places, the Classic City stands strong on the shoulders of those who came before. Tours of the homes are available through reservations made at the Historic Athens Welcome Center, located in the c.1820 Church–Waddel–Brumby House, which is believed to be the oldest home. Restored and furnished to the 1820 time period when this home was the residence of UGA's president, Moses Waddel, it's a great introduction to the city's architectural history. Visit the Welcome Center first and make a game plan for discovery.

Ware–Lyndon Historic House

A rare Italianate-designed home built in 1850, it is listed on the National Register of Historic Places and is part of the Lyndon House Arts Center. It's the only surviving home in the fashionable Athens district of Lickskillet.
211 Hoyt St., 706-613-3623
accgov.com

T. R. R. Cobb House

Built in 1834, the house was a wedding present to Thomas Reade Rootes Cobb from his father-in-law in 1844. This Greek Revival home grew as Cobb's wealth did. He was a Confederate officer and died at the Battle of Fredericksburg. It has been a fraternity house and a boardinghouse. It is now a public museum.
175 Hill St., 706-369-3513
trrrcobbhouse.org

Taylor-Grady House

This Greek Revival mansion was built by Robert Taylor in 1844 as his summer house in Athens and was purchased in 1895 by journalist and orator Henry Grady. It is a backdrop for special events and welcomes guided and self-guided tours.
634 Prince Ave., 706-549-8688
taylorgradyhouse.com

Church–Waddel–Brumby House

Believed to be the oldest home in Athens, it was moved to its current location in 1967. It has been fully restored to its 1820 origin.
Athens Welcome Center
280 E Dougherty St., 706-353-1820
athenswelcomecenter.com

BURN
THROUGH HISTORY
ON THE ANTEBELLUM TRAIL

It all begins in Athens, where southern history moves through every element of the city. From food to music, southern is the vein that flows through everything. Many items on this list are part of the 100-mile trail that extends through seven cities. Explore Athens and then meander south until you reach Macon. Each city's welcome center provides information on the Antebellum Trail which advances through their area. The trail follows Sherman's March to the Sea, including stories of the homes he refused to burn because of their beauty. It is self-guided, so take the trail at your own pace. Download the brochure on the website to start your planning.

antebellumtrail.org

FOLLOW THE ANTEBELLUM TRAIL

Watkinsville
The Eagle Tavern
21 N Main St., 706-769-5197
visitoconee.com

Madison
Heritage Hall & Rose Cottage
115 E Jefferson St., 706-342-4454
visitmadisonga.com

Eatonton
Panola Hall
706-485-7701
visiteatonton.com

Milledgeville
Georgia's Old Capitol & Governor's Mansion
200 W Hancock St.
visitmilledgeville.org

Gray | Old Clinton
Jarrell Plantation State Historic Site
161 W Clinton St., Gray, 478-986-1123
jonescounty.org

Macon
Hay House & Cannonball House
450 Martin Luther King Jr. Blvd., 478-743-1074
visitmacon.org

VISIT THE SON OF THE TREE
THAT OWNS ITSELF

Follow the city's lone cobblestone street off Broad Street near downtown Athens that leads into a residential neighborhood. Up the hill and straight ahead is the tree that owns itself, surrounded by a small chain fence and a stone sharing its story. On land once owned by Colonel William H. Jackson, a University of Georgia professor, stands a white oak tree. He loved it so much that he deeded the tree eight feet of land from each of its sides in perpetuity. The original tree fell in 1942 during a windstorm. It was thought to be 400 years old. The tree that stands now grew from a sapling from the original tree's acorn. It's the only Athens resident who doesn't have to pay taxes.

Corner of South Finley and Dearing Streets

PUT THE EXCEPTIONAL
IN UGA SPECIAL
COLLECTIONS LIBRARIES

Sure, it's a library. In fact, it's a series of three libraries on the University of Georgia campus. Within the three collections live unique photos, documents, manuscripts, and more that tell the history of Georgia. From colonial history to modern music, the galleries provide access to some of the influential and historical documents available. Exhibitions, tours, and other programs are listed on the website. When the Georgia Music Hall of Fame in Macon closed in 2008, artifacts were transferred to its current home in the Special Collection Libraries. With Athens being such a music-driven city, it was the perfect location. Items include B-52s flashy outfits, musical instruments, and boat shoes from Widespread Panic's lead singer John Bell. The library will showcase its music exhibition in 2023.

300 S Hull St., 706-542-7123
libs.uga.edu

HEAR THE STORIES OF ATHENIANS AND THE THINGS THEY DO AFTER THEY DIE
ON THE ATHENS HAUNTED HISTORY WALKING TOUR

There's no denying the power of a good storyteller. And if the eloquent and deep voice of Jeff Clarke delivers the story, that's the cherry on top. Join Clarke for the perfect blend of history, folklore, and a little spooky on the Athens Haunted History Walking Tour. Whether you've lived in Athens all your life or are new to this vibrant city, this tour will educate and enlighten you on everything Athens. With his extensive research and years of collecting local stories, including those strange and supernatural and unexplained, he combined his love of history and crafted a tour of ghostly encounters. The tour will begin and end at the Graduate Hotel. All tours are by appointment only.

The Graduate Hotel
295 E Dougherty St., 706-521-2556
athenshauntedhistory.com

FUN FACT

Jeff Clarke appears as an on-air historian and consultant for *The American Revolution and America: Fact vs. Fiction*. He also was featured on Travel Channel's *Tales of Terror*. Having made his home in Athens for the last 30 years, he understands the vibrant nightlife in the city, plus the equally vibrant afterlife.

WALK THE BIRTHPLACE OF HIGHER EDUCATION
ON NORTH CAMPUS

The charming North Campus inspires with its Greek Revival architecture, stately trees, and beautiful gardens. A cast-iron arch marks the entrance to the University of Georgia, the nation's first chartered university in 1785. Its sprawling lawn leads to the modern campus, and its canopy of trees frame the historic buildings. The chapel, built in 1832 at the cost of $15,000, was the site of the daily service and the bell that signaled the end of classes. The painting *Interior of St. Peter's*, by American George Cooke, measures 17 by 23 feet, and depicts the interior of St. Peter's Basilica in Rome. The Founders Memorial Garden, tucked behind Herty Field, commemorates the 12 founders of the American garden club, established in 1891. There are over 300 species of plants, and it is listed on the National Register of Historic Places. Another slice of heaven on campus.

FUN FACT

Designed after the State of Georgia seal with three columns representing wisdom, justice, and moderation, the Arch is the most iconic symbol of the University of Georgia. Superstition states that only those who have graduated from the university should walk underneath. Don't let that stop you from this must-do photo opportunity. US 78

VISIT THE ICONIC VAUDEVILLE THEATER,
MORTON THEATRE

The Morton Building in downtown Athens anchored "Hot Corner," the commercial center of the Black community in the early 1900s. Built in 1910, it was the first vaudeville theater in the US that was built, owned, and operated by an African American, Monroe Bowers Morton. The four-story building housed offices, but on the second and third floors was the Morton Theatre. Vaudeville and blues performers like Louis Armstrong, Ma Rainey, and Duke Ellington made stops in Athens. Retaining its original gas-lighting outlets, the theater seats 480. Listed on the National Register of Historic Places, the building's renovation transformed the space into a historic community performing-arts center. The Morton Heritage Players, as well as the Athens Creative Theatre and Black Theatrical Ensemble, present contemporary American theater throughout the year.

195 W Washington St., 706-613-3770
mortontheatre.com

PORE OVER WORKS OF LOCAL WRITERS
AT GEORGIA WRITERS MUSEUM

Lovers of words must take a detour to the small town of Eatonton, about 50 miles south. The literary community rejoices with the creation of the Georgia Writers Museum in 2014. Nine of the 70-plus members of the Georgia Writers Hall of Fame (UGA) plied their trade within 30 miles of the museum, and all nine are exhibited in the museum. The exhibits go into detail about their lives and works. Did you know these writers are from the Athens area? Joel Chandler Harris (*Brer Rabbit*). Alice Walker (*The Color Purple*). Terry Kay (*To Dance with the White Dog*). Come see Terry Kay's typewriter on display. Sidney Lanier's flute inspired his poetry like "The Song of the Chattahoochee"; it's on display, too. A great girls' afternoon out is the Meet the Author series, held the first Tuesday of each month. Enjoy brunch, mimosas, and book signings.

109 S Jefferson Ave., Eatonton, 706-991-5119
georgiawritersmuseum.org

TIP
They offer virtual book clubs. No matter where you are, sign up!

DRAW TOGETHER
AT LYNDON HOUSE ARTS CENTER

With hundreds of galleries and museums in the city of Athens, the options are as plentiful as the artwork. The Lyndon House Arts Center offers rotating exhibitions, educational programs, and workshops for young people and adults. Cultural festivals and community events are also held at the Ware–Lyndon Historic House Museum, located next to the center. Youth and adult art classes and camps rotate with the seasons. A variety of art exhibitions fill the calendar; all are free and open to the public. Gallery talks and receptions with exhibiting artists are on the third Thursday of each month. Each year, they have a juried exhibit, as well as a call for artists. Exhibitions are planned years in advance, so check your travel schedule to see what will be available. Local and international artists are featured.

211 Hoyt St., 706-613-3623
accgov.com

TIP

A project sponsored by the Lyndon House Arts Center, Athens Mural Alley is located in the alley between West Clayton and West Washington streets. Take a walk and a camera.

SHELTER THE WATERS
WITH HISTORIC COVERED BRIDGES

A picturesque reminder of the past, covered bridges transfer people back to a simpler time in America. That might be the reason they are sought out by travelers. Two covered bridges remain in the Athens area, and each is worth an afternoon drive. Built in 1897 and moved to its current location in 1924, Elder Mill Covered Bridge is one of only a few functioning bridges in the state. Located in the Watkinsville area, it is the only bridge on the Antebellum Trail. This single-lane, highly trafficked bridge, is 100 feet in length and crosses Rose Creek. Each holiday season, the community drapes Christmas lights along the bridge's side, a photo of which would be an ideal backdrop for your annual Christmas card. Watson Mill Bridge is the longest covered bridge in the state and spans 229 feet across the South Fork River. It is located in Watson Mill Bridge State Park and is a popular destination for river outings, hiking, and horseback riding. Both designs are Town lattice truss systems, held together with wooden pins.

Elder Mill Covered Bridge
1441 Elder Mill Rd., Watkinsville

Watson Mill Bridge State Park
650 Watson Mill Rd., Comer
gastateparks.org

EXPLORE HISTORY
AT THE GEORGIA MUSEUM
OF NATURAL HISTORY

The entire family will be amazed while walking through this facility that chronicles Georgia's natural history, though it's not exclusive to Georgia and the Southeast. The Georgia Museum of Natural History, a research facility on the University of Georgia campus, houses 11 collections that illustrate the story of Georgia, from its ancient past to the present day. These collections represent many thousands of hours of research in a variety of fields of study. The exhibit gallery is open to everyone. Exhibits include botany, earth sciences, archaeology, and more. It is a repository for the preservation of tangible history. It exists to serve as a teaching facility, but its broader goal is outreach and assistance in understanding natural history. The museum houses one of the largest collections of dinosaur bones in the world.

Corner of Cedar Street and East Campus Road, 706-542-1663
naturalhistory.uga.edu

TIP
To schedule a tour or to review specific collections, visit the website and contact the museum.

● ●

SHOPPING
AND FASHION

GRAB EVERYTHING AND THE KITCHEN SINK
AT J & J FLEA MARKET

If you can't find what you're looking for on these 182 acres, it doesn't exist. J & J Flea Market is an iconic venue, well-known to everyone who has visited Athens. It has been going strong since 1988. Open every weekend throughout the year, the market and its vendors sell the new and the old to visitors and locals. There are more than 2,000 vendors, five restaurants, and a farmers market. In addition to outside stalls, it also offers 125,000 square feet of indoor shopping. Find everything from home goods and collectibles to fishing gear. Have something to sell? Book a space online. There are the usual vendors, but new sellers are always welcome. Every weekend offers different items and experiences. Take an afternoon to explore.

11661 Commerce Rd., 706-613-2410
jandjfleamarket.com

GIFT A WORK OF ART
FROM NATTY MICHELLE PAPERIE

A brick-and-mortar storefront isn't needed to turn heads. Artist Natalie Kilgore's unmistakable work on gifts, apparel, and paper is charming. The simplistic, pencil-like, drawn etchings illustrate skylines like Athens and Atlanta. Landmark, mascot, and city etchings decorate candles, stickers and stationery; the product, as well as the art, is limited only by your imagination. These handmade products make the perfect gift for special occasions as well as celebrations for small businesses or just-because moments. Her full line of products, as well as custom-made items, can be ordered on her website. Many small businesses in Athens carry some of her products. The Athens skyline on a personalized notepad is delightful.

nattymichellepaperie.com

TIP

Jittery Joe's carries the Athens skyline mugs.

TREASURE YOUR HANDMADE LEATHER BELT
FROM MASADA LEATHER

It's the scent of leather as you enter the studio that tells of its timeless and classic beauty. At Masada Leather, simply walking in the door treats the senses to the unmistakable, handmade craftmanship of leather. For three decades, Irvin Alhadeff has been crafting fine leather goods. He started as a hobby during his days at Florida State University, and the passion turned into a profession. He says making a belt is easy, but making one that will last a lifetime takes patience and precision. Masada's reputation for handmade bridle-leather belts, wallets, and Italian leather bags draws fans from around the state and has created a recipe for success and longevity. Order your perfect belt, but take the time to visit the shop and watch the master at work.

675 Pulaski St., 706-521-5632
masadaleather.com

PICK THE CREAM OF THE CROP
AT ATHENS FARMERS MARKET

It's a weekly event for locals. Gather at the farmers market and plan weekly meals from the freshest of ingredients that also support area farmers. This gathering connects people to the roots of their food. All food is organically grown, and the prepared foods are handmade without dyes or preservatives. Stop by for breakfast on Saturday and dinner on Wednesday. Children are entertained at the children's booth while parents shop. A local chef prepares a dish from produce found at the market. And everything happens as live music provides the soundtrack. Started by the community and for the community, the goal continues to be establishing the food connection.

Bishop Park
Saturdays, March–December
705 Sunset Dr.

Downtown, Creature Comforts Brewing
Wednesdays, April–October
271 W Hancock Ave.

athensfarmersmarket.net

SHOWCASE THE ARTISTS
AT OCONEE CULTURAL ARTS
FOUNDATION (OCAF)

Affectionally called Artland of Georgia, the small community of Watkinsville thrives on the shoulders of the artist community. It has more artists per capita than any other town in the state. Throughout the city and county, you'll see installations and sculptures standing tall on landscapes. The foundation began in the mid-1940s with the dream of five people highlighting the arts in Oconee. Decades later, it became a nonprofit arts charity. A 1902 four-room schoolhouse serves as event space and the cornerstone of art activity; it has been renovated and is alive with ongoing exhibits, studios, classes, and performances. Its annual event, Perspectives: A Georgia Pottery Invitational, is a calling-card for artists around the Southeast to showcase their work. Complete your Christmas list at their holiday market.

34 School St., Watkinsville, 706-769-4565
ocaf.com

POTTER'S PARADISE
Happy Valley Pottery
1210 Carson Graves Rd., Watkinsville, 706-769-5922
happyvalleypottery.com

Lori Breedlove
1051 Rose Creek Dr., Watkinsville
rosecreekpottery.com

Michele Dross
515 King Ave.
micheledross.com

Regina Mandell
1063 W Hancock Ave.
forgedandfound.net

Matt Powelson
2980 Greensboro Hwy.,Watkinsville
321-pottery.com

Zuzka Vaclavik
159 Oneta St.
zuzkavaclavik.com

BAG VINTAGE AND MODERN TREASURES
AT WOMEN'S BOUTIQUES

From the heart of downtown and beyond, boutiques are bursting with the latest styles and trends for women. From funky to functional, classic to boho, designer to handmade, buyers curate collections to fill, first, shopping bags, then closets. Most boutiques are female-owned, and the ladies value sharing their personal flair and style with customers. From a Dolly Parton facsimile to a high school sports team chant, shirts capture the essence and the message of the 21st-century female. You'll find equal attention being offered to the college-age customer as well as to the mature woman. Finding the ideal clothing or accessory is effortless with the store choices that are available. Many offer online experiences, but where's the fun in that?

ON YOUR MARK, SHOP!

Agora Vintage
Open by appointment, Tuesday–Saturday
Designer clothing and accessories
279 E Broad St., 706-255-2632
agoravintageshop.com

Heery's
195 College Ave., 706-543-0702
heerys.com

Community
260 N Jackson St., 706-316-2067
shopcommunityathens.com

Cheeky Peach
160 W Clayton St., 706-353-1322
shopcheekypeach.com

Dynamite Clothing
143 N Jackson St.
shopdynamiteathens.com

Empire South
166 W Clayton St., 706-424-2467
2 S Main St., Watkinsville, 706-567-8493
shopempiresouth.com

Wildflower
1430 Capital Ave., #105, Watkinsville
wildflowerclothingandhome.com

DRESS
LIKE A NATIONAL CHAMPION

How 'Bout Them Dawgs! If you are an Athenian, you have a T-shirt or sweatshirt emblazoned with the "G." If you are an alum or current student, your wardrobe is constructed around the red and black. Everyone can tell a story of a tattered college jersey or T-shirt worn decades after its purchase. The imprinted T or sweat is a requisite for any die-hard Southeastern Conference (SEC) football fan. And for the first time in 40 years, the shirt speaks to history. Acquire a legendary piece of clothing that proclaims, finally, in 2021, the Georgia Bulldogs are college football national champions again. To say Athens loves its home team is an understatement. And as rumored, yes, we do bleed red and black, and we always do it in Bulldogs T's and sweats.

POWER-PURCHASE
AT EPIPHANY

As far as window shopping goes, Epiphany nails it. It's the building that will grab your attention. Then, the artfully constructed displays will have you wearing the dress in your mind's eye before you walk in. However, the shop is much more than its contents; it's a mission. Outward beauty mirrors inner beauty, and women at Epiphany help women discover effortless style that reflects confidence. More than that, the business provides owners Dara and Paul a platform for giving to the poor, underserved, and vulnerable in the Athens community and around the world. Every purchase benefits local and global charity partners. Once a missionary in Ukraine, Dara developed a passion for helping orphaned kids. She also loved clothes and Jesus. How do you combine these? She had an epiphany, and the rest is history.

294 W Washington St., 706-395-6904
epiphanyathens.com

RELISH NATURE
AT R. WOOD STUDIO

One of the largest studio potteries in the US, r. wood studio speaks to the beauty of nature and all its inspiration. Collectors seek Rebecca Wood's work, and a visit to Athens allows visitors to see the process and purchase their very own collectible. Located in an old produce warehouse in the Carr's Hill neighborhood, the studio constructs small batches and specialty pieces that are limited editions, designed and handmade by Wood's six-artist team. A painter-turned-potter, Wood is inspired by southern beauty in gardens and woods which in turn begets her tangible art. Get to know Wood and her talent by signing up for a digital Ikebana workshop, the Japanese art of flower arranging. While signing up on the website, survey the shop and pick out your next purchase.

450 Georgia Dr., 706-613-8525
rwoodstudio.com

FUN FACT

You can order r. wood studio items through *Sundance Catalog*, the stylish western shop created by Robert Redford

SHOP FOR THE GENTLEMEN
AT ONWARD RESERVE

Feel the sense of the classic the moment you walk in the door. Inspired by a hunting trip to Onward, Mississippi, and the Teddy Roosevelt "Teddy Bear" story, founder TJ Callaway bases every piece of clothing, every accessory, every element in the store on authenticity. Callaway designs each season's collection, and selects other brands to showcase, with the authentic lifestyle in mind. The upscale shop outfits the man who chooses style as his main accessory. Unique finds include UGA needlepoint cufflinks, alligator wallets, and carry-on cocktail kits for air travel. Bulldogs boxers, shirts, and hats overflow in the front of the store, and these, plus all the unique finds, draw people in daily. On game day, the crowded shop feels like a fraternity.

146 E Clayton St., 706-543-0106
onwardreserve.com

TIP
Stop in at Onward Reserve before any home game for complimentary mimosas and beer in their faux living room.

READ A STORY
AT AVID BOOKSHOP

Indigo blue frames its rich discourse inside. Avid Bookshop is a jewel in the city's crown that has showcased the classics and introduced local authors for over a decade. Fiercely independent, Avid shares diverse voices with Athens, taking pride in curated collections chosen specifically for the community. The small space with intimate nooks offers multiple shelves overflowing with paperback and hardcover books chosen by familiar faces. They believe books change lives, and that influences book choices and events. Doing what a big-box or online shop cannot do, Avid brings readers together, supports the community economy, and promotes a local culture. It's personal. You can browse their inventory and staff picks online, but they hope you'll come inside this charming space. Readings, book signings, poetry nights, children's story times, and workshops are usual happenings.

1662 S Lumpkin St., 706-850-2843
avidbookshop.com

BEGIN
THE HOLIDAY SEASON
AT ATHENS HOLIDAY MARKET

Spending time in Athens during the holiday season is the perfect time for taking care of your holiday gift-giving for Christmas, Hanukkah, or Kwanzaa. Not only are you supporting local artisans, but you're also uncovering a personal gift that will be timeless and unique. Holiday markets take place over multiple weekends from November through December at different locations throughout the community. There are some markets which offer specific items like pottery or art. However, the majority of holiday fairs provide smorgasbords of crafts, jewelry, paper goods, bath and body products, and so much more. You'll stock up on gifts for others, and assuredly, you'll find something to take home for yourself. Enjoy the food and drink available for shoppers. Don't forget to stop in at the State Botanical Garden of Georgia gift shop for the botanical gifts.

TIP
The Athens Creatives Directory and Visit Athens website update markets with additions and changes. Check the website before planning your shopping trip. visitathensga.com, athenscreatives.directory

MARKET ROUNDUP

West Broad Farmers Market Holiday Market
300 S Rocksprings St., 706-765-4020
athenslandtrust.org

Small Business Saturday Holiday Fair
Saturday after Thanksgiving
Athentic Brewing Co
108 Park Ave., 706-850-6252

Southern Star Studio Holiday Market
180 Cleveland Ave.
southernstarsstudioathens.com

Holiday Market at Flicker Theatre and Bar
263 W Washington St.
flickertheatreandbar.com

Athens Holiday Market at Big City Bread Café
393 N Finley St.
bigcitybreadcafe.com

Ho Down X at Southern Brewing Company
231 Collins Industrial Blvd., 706-548-7183
sobrewco.com

Indie South Fair: Holiday Hooray!
470 Hawthorne Ave., 706-850-0644
theindiesouth.com

Tiny ATH Gallery: Holi-LADDER-Day Market
174 Cleveland Ave.
tinyathgallery.com

FIND YOUR FAVORITE THINGS
AT INDIE SOUTH

It's a handmade movement, and it's not leaving town. What started as a makeshift shop in Serra Jaggar's home morphed into a concrete platform where local artists sell their wares. There were once-in-a-while festivals, workshops, markets, and gatherings, but now it lives on Hawthorne Avenue, filled with a wealth of individual expressions. Jaggar's eye for the eclectic and devotion to the small business celebrates the handmade. Her Handmade Markets pop up each year and welcome the community to become involved, as buyers and sellers. The Abnormal Bazaar, Springtacular, and the Holiday Hooray might solve your gift-buying dilemmas for the year. If you visit the store, make time for a three-card mini tarot reading with Jaggar. Longer readings are available with appointment.

470 Hawthorne Ave., 706-850-0644
theindiesouth.com

STEP INTO THE BEAUTY
OF STEEL + PLANK

Opposites do attract. STEEL + PLANK creates modern furniture with sleek angles and inviting textures. The showroom feels more like a living room, with sofas constructed with hues of gray fabric and coffee cups that balance on legs of clay. It's the simplicity that grabs. Architect turned furniture designer Kelly Bishop, along with the fabrication studio Very Dark Gray, create custom pieces as individual as you are. Located in the close-knit Pulaski neighborhood, the furniture is showcased with products produced by local artists. Soap. Ceramics. Lighting. Baskets. Art. Through online pop-ups and in-person collaborations, seasonal gatherings bring makers and the community together. Visit during the weekend and enjoy a cup of tea as you browse the space. Don't miss this elegant, simple, and timeless experience.

675 Pulaski St., #200, 706-850-7980
steelandplank.com

ACTIVITIES
BY SEASON

SPRING

SUMMER

FALL

WINTER

• •

Lumberjaxe

University of Georgia North Campus Lawn

SUGGESTED
ITINERARIES

GAME DAY

Dress like a National Champion, 120

Walk the Birthplace of Higher Education on North Campus, 104

Ring the Chapel Bell on North Campus after
  a Bulldogs Win, 90

Count the Dawg Statues, 88

Welcome the Horseplay at Southern Cross Guest Ranch, 82

Toss a Football on Herty Field, 76

Stand Tall with the Iron Horse, 91

Tailgate at a UGA Home Football Game, 64

Strut the Dawg Walk with the Football Players
  and Dawg Nation into Sanford Stadium on Game Day, 74

Start with a Side of Georgia Peach French Toast
  at Mama's Boy, 6

Drink In a Rooftop View at Georgia Theatre or Hybar, 14

Be First at Last Resort Grill, 36

LATE NIGHT IS DATE NIGHT

Eat a Blue-Plate Special in the Picasso Room at Five and Ten, 2

Drink In a Rooftop View at Georgia Theatre or Hybar, 14

Wet Your Whistle with a Peanuts & Coke Cocktail at the Place, 19

Carve into a Filet Mignon at Porterhouse Grill, 9

Catch a Rising Star at Georgia Theatre, 49

Chuck an Axe and Chug a Beer at Lumberjaxe, 78

Take In a Broadway Show at the Classic Center, 57

Picture Inspiration at the Georgia Museum of Art, 92

Hear the Stories of Athenians and the Things They Do after They Die on the Athens Haunted History Walking Tour, 102

Enjoy Classic Crawfish Etouffee at George's Lowcountry Table, 25

FAMILY OUTINGS

Say Yes to Cookie Dough at Alumni Cookie Dough, 3

Order a Clocked!Burger and PBJ Shake at Clocked, 12

Indulge in Creamy Confections at Condor Chocolates, 23

Praise Local Farmers at Heirloom Café and Fresh Market, 24

Devour a Steak Cubano at Cali N Tito's, 26

Chase a Game and Drink a Darth Roast at the Rook & Pawn Board Game Café, 29

Order (at Least) a Half Dozen Potato Donuts at Café Racer Coffee + Donuts, 34

• •

HISTORICAL

• •

GIRLS' WEEKEND

INDEX

● ●